Pedal Power

Contents

Introduction	2
Riding for Work	4
Racing	9
Riding for Fun	12
Index	16

Carol Krueger

Introduction

Around the world, many people ride bicycles.

China

Holland

Africa

People use bicycles for work, they ride bicycles in races and they ride bicycles for fun.

CYCLE FACT

A bicycle has two wheels.

Bi means *two* and **cycle** means *wheel*.

Riding for Work

In some cities, people ride bicycles to pick up and deliver packages. Bikes can be faster than cars on busy streets.

Here is someone in Australia delivering the mail by bike.

Here are some people in Africa carrying bananas to market by bike.

Some people sell things from their bicycles.

Here is someone selling ice cream from his tricycle. The tricycle has a freezer box on the front wheels that keeps the ice cream cold.

CYCLE FACT

A tricycle has three wheels.

Tri means *three* and **cycle** means *wheel*.

In some countries, a tricycle can be a taxi.

 This taxi tricycle is called a rickshaw.

CYCLE FACT

People paint their rickshaws with beautiful patterns so they will stand out in the traffic.

CYCLE FACT

In India, some children are taken to school in bike vans.

▲ Here are some children going to school by rickshaw.

Racing

Some bicycles are made for racing.

 a mountain bike

 a racing bike

Racing bikes are faster than other bicycles. They are light and are designed for speed.

CYCLE FACT

On a racing bike, riders lean forward so they can ride faster and not be slowed down by the wind.

Mountain bikes are strong. People ride mountain bikes up hills and across country where other bicycles can't go.

CYCLE FACT

A triathlon is a very hard race. The racers first swim, then ride their bicycles, and then run.

Riding for Fun

People also ride bicycles for fun.

▲ Here is a clown riding a tiny bicycle.

CYCLE FACT

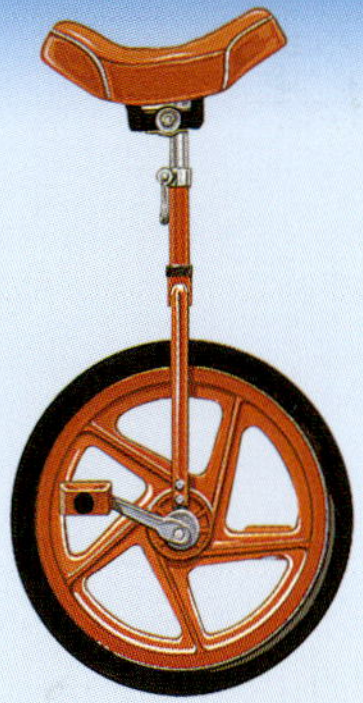

A unicycle has only one wheel.

Uni means *one* and **cycle** means *wheel*.

◀ Here is a clown riding a unicycle.

Lots of people can ride this bicycle because it is the longest bicycle in the world.

It was made in Italy.
Nearly forty people can ride it – but it's hard to go round a corner.

Index

Africa   2, 5
Australia   4
bicycle   3
bike van   8
China   2
clowns   12–13
fun   3, 12–15
Holland   2
India   8
Italy   15
mountain bike   9, 11

racing   3, 9–11
racing bike   9, 10
rickshaw   7, 8
taxi   7, 8
triathlon   11
tricycle   6, 7, 8
unicycle   13
work   3–8
world's longest bike   14